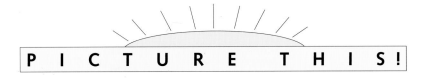

Toys

Karen Bryant-Mole

RIGBY
INTERACTIVE
LIBRARY

This edition ©1997 Rigby Education
Published by Rigby Interactive Library,
an imprint of Reed Educational & Professional Publishing
500 Coventry Lane
Crystal Lake, IL 60014

Printed in China
01 00 99 98 97
10 9 8 7 6 5 4 3 2 1

Library of Congress Cataloging-in-Publication Data

Bryant-Mole, Karen.
  Toys/Karen Bryant-Mole.
    p. cm.—(Picture this!)   Includes index.
  Summary: Text and photgraphs identify various types of toys, including wheels, moving toys, musical toys, and outdoor toys.
    ISBN 1-57572-057-4 (lib. bdg.)
    1. Toys—Juvenile literatur: [1. Toys.] I. Title.
    II. Series.
GV1218.5.B79   1997   96-37243
790.1'33—dc21   CIP
                                             AC

Text designed by Jean Wheeler

Acknowledgments
The publisher would like to thank the following for permission to reproduce photographs.
Eye Ubiquitous, p. 8 (left); Tony Stone Images, p. 23 (right); Andre Perlstein/Zefa, p. 8 (right); p. 9 (left and back cover), p. 9 (right), p. 22, p. 23 (left).

> **Note to the Reader**
> Some words in this book may be new to you.
> You may look them up in the glossary on page 24.

Visit Rigby's Education Station® on the World Wide Web at http://www.rigby.com

Contents

What Toys are Made of

Toys can be made from a lot of different materials.

These cars and trucks are made from wood.

These animals are
made from plastic.

Texture

The word texture means how something feels.

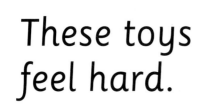

These toys feel hard.

These toys feel soft.

Wheels

These toys have wheels.

toy car

skateboard

tricycle

You can move fast on toys with wheels.

Moving Toys

How would you
make these
toys move?

pull

throw

push

wind up

11

Batteries

These toys need batteries to work.

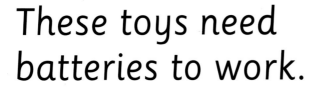

lightboard

flashlight

throw

push

wind up

11

Batteries

These toys need batteries to work.

lightboard

flashlight

remote-contolled car

Toys with batteries
can be turned on and off.

Musical Toys

These toys make different types of sounds.

maracas

trumpet

bells

drum

They are
all toy
musical
instruments.

Building Toys

Some toys can be used
to build or make things.

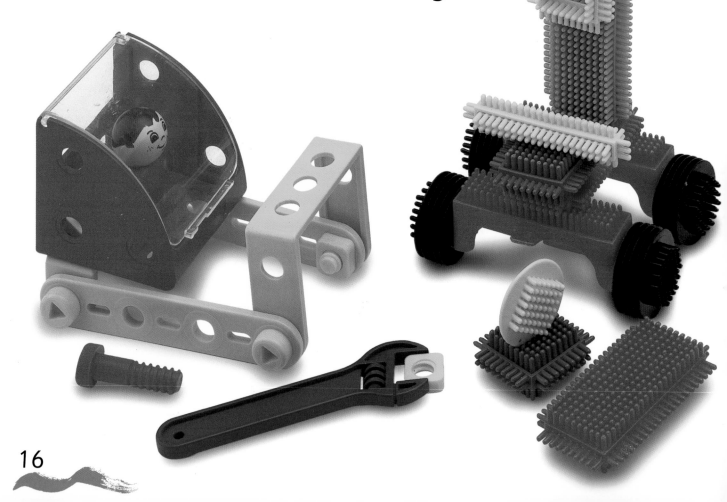

Toys like these are
sometimes called construction toys.

Jigsaw Puzzles

Jigsaw puzzles can be easy or hard.

Which of these
puzzles looks the easiest?

Pretend Play

These toys look like things that you may have at home.

iron

toaster

food

telephone

Outdoor Toys

Some toys should be played with outdoors.

playhouse

bouncer

kite

Pail and shovel

Glossary

batteries Objects that store electricity and are used to make things work. 12

construction toys Toys that are made to build or make things and that look like real tools or building machines. 17

jigsaw puzzles Group of different-shaped pieces that fit together to make a picture. 18

materials What things are made from. 4

musical instruments Things that you can make music with. 15

Index